Loanends
Sabbeth School.

Presented to

Louise Dunlop

For Perfect

Attendance

1985 - 86

PICKERING & INGLIS LTD.   PRINTED IN GREAT BRITAIN

CONTENTS

First published in 1983
Reprinted in 1985

Published by Deans International Publishing
52–54 Southwark Street, London, SE1 1UA
A division of The Hamlyn Publishing Group Limited
London · New York · Sydney · Toronto

Text and illustrations Copyright © Deans International Publishing,
a division of The Hamlyn Publishing Group Limited, 1983

ISBN 0 603 00353 2

Printed and Bound in Great Britain

OLD TESTAMENT

Bible Stories
for Children

Retold by Nancy Martin

illustrated by Gwen Green

God Made the World

We live in the world which God created and it is very beautiful. First, God gave us light so that we could see the beauty. He called this light-time—Day. He also gave us the dark. He called this dark-time—Night.

This was the first day and God liked it.

Next, God made a huge space between the waters below and the rain clouds above. Then there was sea and sky. The sky held the rain clouds a long way up above the sea.

This was the second day and God liked what he had done that day. But the earth was covered by sea, so God said:

'Let the water under the sky be gathered in one place and let the ground appear.' And he called the ground—Land.

There were no plants or trees, so God said:

'Let the land produce trees and plants with fruit and seeds,' and the earth looked bright with lovely colours.

This was the third day and God knew this was good.

Then God put lights in the sky to separate the day and the night. There were twinkling stars and two great lights. The greater light shone in the day to give warmth and brightness, and the lesser gave light at night. God called them—Sun and Moon.

This was the fourth day and this also was good.

The next day God said:

'Let the water team with living creatures, and let birds fly above the earth and across the sky.'

This was the fifth day and God saw it was good.

God wanted more life on the land so the next day he created many different creatures.

God saw all that he had done and it was good.

There was just one other thing he wanted to do. He wanted to make man. So he created man in his own image and he said:

'Be fruitful and increase in number.'

God looked at everything he had done and saw all that he had made was good.

This was the sixth day.

Then God rested on the seventh day when his work of creation was completed. And he blessed the seventh day.

GENESIS, *chapters 1, 2*

God's Garden

The man whom God had created, he called Adam. He gave him a beautiful garden where he could live and work, and said to him:

'You are free to eat from any tree in the garden, but you must not eat from the tree of the knowledge of good and evil, for if you eat of it you will surely die.'

So Adam went to live in the garden.

Then God said:

'It is not good for man to be alone. I will make a helper suitable for him.'

So he created a woman and she was called Eve.

One day a serpent, one of the creatures in the garden, tempted Eve to eat the forbidden fruit from the tree of the knowledge of good and evil. But Eve told the serpent that God had said they were not to eat the fruit from that tree.

The serpent told her that God only said that because he knew if they ate it they would be like him, knowing good and evil.

Eve gazed at the fruit on the tree and it looked very good. Slowly she stretched out her hand. She picked some of the fruit and ate it. Then she gave some to Adam.

'Where are you?' called God. 'Have you eaten from the tree that I commanded you not to eat from?'

Adam and Eve had to confess that they had. Sin and wrongdoing had entered into God's world, so God sent them out of the beautiful garden and punished them.

GENESIS, *chapters 2, 3*

Cain Kills Abel

Adam and Eve had two sons, the elder was named Cain and the younger was called Abel. Abel looked after the flocks while Cain worked on the land.

One day they each brought an offering to God. Cain brought something he had grown while Abel brought some of the finest of the lambs he had reared. Abel's offering pleased God—he had brought the best he had. But Cain's offering did not give God much pleasure.

Cain was very angry because God did not like his gift and God knew this. He knew too that he was jealous of his brother.

'Why are you angry?' asked God. 'If you do what is right you and your gift will be acceptable, and if you are tempted to do wrong you must resist that temptation.'

One day, Cain said to Abel:

'Let's go out to the field.'

They went out together but Cain did not try to get rid of his bad feelings, as God had told him to. Instead he became so angry and bad-tempered that he attacked Abel and killed him.

Cain knew he had sinned against his brother and against God before God told him so. Then God told Cain that his punishment would be to leave his home and become a restless wanderer.

So Cain left home and he was very unhappy because he knew he had done wrong and it had happened because he had not obeyed God's command.

GENESIS, *chapter 4*

9

The Flood

More and more people were born into God's world but most of them did things which were wrong and God was very displeased with them. There was one man who did please God. His name was Noah and one day God said to him:

'I am going to bring floodwater on the earth and everything will be destroyed.'

And God told Noah that he wanted him to make an ark which would float on the water. God said it was to be big enough for Noah and his family to live in it with two each of all the animals.

'You are to store in the ark every kind of food that is to be eaten by you all,' said God.

Noah did exactly what God told him. When the rain started and water began to cover the earth, Noah and all his family were warm and dry in their new home with the animals which God had told him to take with them.

The rain fell for forty days and forty nights until the mountains even were covered with water. But the ark continued to float. When at last the rain stopped, the wind blew and the water slowly went down. Then Noah opened the window in the ark and let out a raven. The bird flew backwards and forwards but there was nowhere outside for it to perch. Next Noah sent out a dove, but the dove came back too.

Noah waited awhile before sending the dove out again. This time it flew back with an olive leaf in its beak and Noah knew that very soon the ark would rest on dry land.

Then God told Noah to bring everyone out of the ark. When they were all safe, Noah built an altar and made a sacrifice to thank God for his care of them. Then God made a promise to Noah:

'Never again will I destroy all living creatures as I have done. So long as the earth endures, seedtime and harvest, cold and heat, summer and winter, day and night will never cease.'

And God set a rainbow in the sky and said:

'This is the sign of the promise I have established between me and all life on the earth.'

When we see the rainbow we remember God's promise made all those years ago.

GENESIS, *chapters 6, 7, 8*

Abraham's Greatest Test

One of the men who was born and grew up after the flood was named Abraham. He was a good and wise man who tried to do what God commanded. Because God had important work for Abraham to do he tested him many times, but the hardest test came when his son Isaac was growing up. One day, God said to him:

'Take your son, your only son Isaac, whom you love, and go to Moriah. Sacrifice him there as a burnt offering on one of the mountains I will tell you about.'

Abraham loved his son dearly but he put God's commands first. The next morning he got up early, cut some wood for the fire he must make, saddled his donkey, and set off with two of his servants and Isaac on the three days' journey to the place that God had told him about. When they arrived Abraham said to his servants:

'Stay here with the donkey while I and the boy go over there. We will worship and then we will come back to you.'

On the way Isaac said to his father:

'The fire and the wood are here but where is the lamb for the burnt offering?'

'God will provide the lamb for the burnt offering, my son,' replied Abraham.

When they arrived at the place Abraham built an altar and laid Isaac on it. Abraham was just about to make his greatest sacrifice when he heard his name called:

'Abraham! Abraham!'

'Here I am,' said Abraham.

The voice came again:

'Do not lay a hand on the boy. Do not do anything to him. Now I know you fear God because you have not withheld from me your son.'

Looking around Abraham saw a ram caught in a bush, so he took it and offered God the ram instead of his son.

'Because you did not withhold your son, your only son,' said God, 'I will surely bless you and make your descendants as numerous as the sand on the seashore.'

And Abraham became a father to a great nation.

GENESIS, *chapter 22*

Jacob Gets the Blessing

Isaac grew up and had two sons. The first was called Esau and the second Jacob, but Esau was his father's favourite.

One day, when Isaac was old and could not see very well, he said to his elder son:

'Go and hunt some wild game and prepare the food I like, then bring it to me and I will give you my blessing.'

It was the custom for fathers to give their elder son a blessing before they died.

Isaac's wife heard what he said to Esau. As soon as Esau had gone she called her younger son, Jacob, and told him what she had heard.

'Go out to the flock and bring me two choice goats,' she said. 'Then I will prepare some tasty food for your father. You can take it to him so that he may give you his blessing before he dies.'

'But my brother is a hairy man and I have smooth skin,' said Jacob. 'What if my father touches me?'

But his mother persuaded him to do as she asked. So Jacob fetched the goats and took them to his mother. When she had cooked them she covered his neck and his hands with the hairy goats' skin. Then she gave him some of Esau's clothes to wear.

When Jacob was ready he went to his father.

'You have been very quick,' said his father. 'Come near, that I can touch you to know whether you really are my son Esau.'

When he had touched Jacob he said:

'The voice is the voice of Jacob but the hands are the hands of Esau.'

Jacob gave his father the food he had brought for him and asked for his blessing. But his father was still puzzled. Was this his elder or his younger son he wondered?

'Come here, my son,' he said, 'and kiss me.'

When Jacob went close to him Isaac caught the smell of Esau's clothes and he seemed satisfied. So he blessed Jacob.

But when Esau returned and found that Jacob had been given his blessing he was very angry. He was so angry that Jacob had to leave home and go to another place to live. He was very sad and very lonely but when he lay down in the open country to sleep that night he had a dream in which he learnt that God was still with him.

Later he married and had sons. The next story is about his favourite son, who was named Joseph.

GENESIS, *chapters 27, 28*

Joseph the Dreamer

Joseph was a dreamer. Not only did he dream but he could remember his dreams and explain them. He could also interpret other people's dreams.

One night, Pharaoh, King of Egypt, dreamt that he was standing by the River Nile when seven fat cows came and grazed among the reeds. In his dream he also saw seven ugly thin cows come and stand beside the fat cows, and these thin cows ate the seven fat ones!

Then the King woke up but soon he fell asleep again and had another dream. This time he saw seven heads of corn. They all looked good and healthy but then seven other heads of corn sprouted. They were thin and scorched by the east wind. Just as the thin cows had eaten the fat ones so these thin ears of corn ate all the good corn.

The King's dreams seemed so real to him that he was sure they must have some meaning, so he sent for the wise men and the magicians and told them about the dreams. But they could not tell him the meaning.

Then his cup-bearer remembered Joseph. So he said to the king:

'When the chief baker and I were in prison there was a man there who could interpret dreams. His name is Joseph.'

So Pharaoh sent for Joseph and asked him to interpret the dreams.

'God will give you the answer,' said Joseph.

Then Pharaoh repeated his dreams to Joseph. When he had finished speaking Joseph said:

'God is telling you that you are going to have a very good harvest for the next seven years, but after that there will be seven years of famine.'

Joseph went on to tell Pharaoh that he must find someone to put in charge of storing the harvest from the good years for use in the bad years.

The King thought the advice was good and he said to Joseph:

'I am putting you in charge of the whole land of Egypt.'

Joseph had suffered a number of misfortunes. He had been sold by his brothers because they were jealous of him, he had been falsely accused, and Pharaoh had put him in prison. But God had been with him and now his own dreams were to come true, as Pharaoh's did.

GENESIS, *chapter 41*

Moses–the Baby Who Survived

When Pharaoh discovered that many Hebrew boys were being born, he made a law that these boys must be thrown into the river as soon as they were born. The mothers were heartbroken at this cruel command but they were afraid to disobey the King.

One woman was determined to save her baby son so she hid him for three months. She knew she could not go on hiding him, so she took a strong basket and coated it with tar and pitch to keep out water. Then, very carefully, she laid her baby in the basket and took it to the river bank. There she hid the basket among the reeds.

Her little girl went with her and she told her to watch and see what happened. Then the woman went home and the baby's sister stood a little away from the river and waited to see if anyone would find her brother.

Presently the King's daughter came along with her slave-girl. The woman was just going to bathe in the river when she saw the baby in the basket. He was crying and she felt sorry for him.

'This is one of the Hebrew boys,' she said, and she knew that her father had said none must live.

The baby's sister came forward.

'Shall I go and get one of the Hebrew women to come and nurse the baby for you?' the girl asked.

'Yes. Go,' said Pharaoh's daughter.

The little girl ran quickly and brought her mother back to the river.

'Take this baby and nurse him for me,' said Pharaoh's daughter, not knowing that this was the mother of the baby.

So the baby's mother took him and brought him up. When he was grown up she took him to the King's daughter and he became her son. She called him Moses, because she drew him out of the water. We shall hear more about him in the next story.

EXODUS, *chapter 2*

A Journey and a Miracle

Moses became the leader of God's people, the Israelites. Although Moses was in favour with Pharaoh, the Israelites were ill-treated. They were commanded to kill their firstborn boys, and were made slaves to the Egyptians. If they did not work hard they were beaten.

Moses spoke to God about this and God said he would punish the Egyptians.

Soon after that the children of the Egyptians began to die and so did the firstborn of their animals. Pharaoh was very angry.

'Go!' he said to Moses. 'Take your people out of Egypt.'

And Moses knew that God would be with them. So they loaded their camels and set out on the long journey across the desert. Moses led them to the place that God had told him, where they were to camp that night. The Red Sea was in front of them and they had no means of crossing it. They were shut in between mountains and the sea. But that was not all that troubled them.

As soon as they had left Egypt Pharaoh began to wish he had not let them go for he had lost his cheap labour. So he sent his army after them.

When the Israelites saw the army approaching they were frightened. There seemed no way of escape and they were angry with Moses for leading them there.

'We'd rather have stayed in Egypt as slaves than die in the desert,' they said.

So Moses talked to God again. God had told him to take the people on this journey and he trusted God to help them.

'Take your staff and stretch out your hand across the sea,' said God.

The wind blew and the cloud which had been in front of them moved in between them and the Egyptians so that they could not see each other. As Moses stretched out his hand the wind blew from the east so strongly that the sea was divided, leaving a pathway to the other side.

Then the people were joyful. They took their possessions and set off in a long trail between the high banks of water on either side of them.

But all was not well yet. If they could cross so could the Egyptians and they came charging across. But they were soon in difficulty. The wheels of their chariots came off and they began to panic.

'The Lord is fighting for them,' they said fearfully. 'Let's go back.'

And they turned away, but the Israelites got safely across. They stood looking in wonder as the wind dropped and the water flowed back, covering the pathway they had just walked on and drowning the Egyptians.

EXODUS, *chapters 13, 14*

Blow the Trumpets!

One day a large army of Midianites came riding through southern Israel on their camels. They looked very fierce and the Israelites were terrified as they watched them settle in the city of Gaza. Gideon, who was afraid the Midianites would take his family's wheat, was threshing it under a tree out of sight of the enemy, when God spoke to him. God called Gideon to be the leader of his people and to drive out the invaders. So Gideon gathered a great army of 32,000 men to fight off the enemy.

But God said to him:

'You have too many men. Send away all who are afraid.'

When Gideon told his men what God had said 22,000 of them went away.

'Take the 10,000 who are left and go down to the water,' said God.

Gideon watched as 300 of the men scooped up the water and lapped it from their hands. The others got down on their knees to drink.

God spoke to Gideon again and said:

'With the 300 men who lapped the water I will save you from the Midianites.'

Then God told Gideon to go down near the camp but if he was afraid to go alone he could take his servant with him. When the two men drew near, they heard a man telling his friend about a dream which his companion understood to mean that the Israelites were going to defeat them. Gideon was afraid no more and returned to do all that God had told him to do.

He gave his men trumpets and jars with torches inside. Then he divided them into three companies, 100 men in each.

'Watch me and follow my lead,' he said.

He led them to a high place which surrounded the camp. When they were all in position they gave a great shout. Then all 300 men blew hard on their trumpets at the same time. They smashed the jars they were holding and they held aloft their torches in their left hands and their trumpets in their right hands.

'A sword for the Lord and for Gideon,' they shouted.

They made so much noise that it appeared as though a great army had surrounded the Midianites, who fled in terror and confusion.

Gideon, by obeying God, had defeated the powerful Midianite army.

JUDGES, *chapter 7*

Ruth and Naomi

There are all kinds of stories in the Bible. This one is a love story.

Naomi's home was in Bethlehem but she had been living in a strange country with her husband and two sons because there was a famine in her own country. Then everything seemed to go wrong. First her husband and then her two sons died and Naomi was left with her two daughters-in-law, Orpah and Ruth.

Naomi wanted to return to her own country and Ruth and Orpah set off with her. But now *they* were leaving *their* homes, so Naomi said to them:

'Go back each to your mother's home so that you may find another husband.'

Neither of the women wanted to leave Naomi to go on alone but at last Orpah was persuaded to return. But Ruth loved Naomi and had come to love the God of Israel so she begged to be allowed to go with her.

'Beseech me not to leave you,' she said. 'Where you go I will go and where you stay I will stay. Your people will be my people, your God my God.'

So they went on together to Bethlehem where they had a good welcome, for Naomi was very popular.

The barley harvest was just beginning and Naomi and Ruth had hardly enough money to buy food. So Ruth begged to be allowed to go and gather up the grain which the harvesters left behind when reaping. The man who owned the field was named Boaz and he liked Ruth. She worked hard and he encouraged her to join the harvesters as they rested at midday.

That evening Naomi asked Ruth where she had been gleaning.

'I worked with Boaz,' said Ruth.

'He is my close relative,' said Naomi, and she was very happy for Ruth to get to know him. Perhaps Boaz would marry Ruth—that would make them all happy. Boaz was an important man in the country and a good man and Naomi knew he would make Ruth a good husband.

Ruth, too, liked Boaz and the more she saw of him the more she liked him. Then, one day, when the harvest was gathered in, Boaz announced to all the people that he and Ruth were to be married. Everyone was very pleased because they liked Ruth. They were even happier when Ruth had a son who was called Obed. He, in turn, had a son named Jesse who later became the father of David, so Ruth became the great grandmother of David. You will find two stories about David in this book.

RUTH

25

You Called Me

Earlier in this book there is a story about a baby boy who was found by a princess. His name was Moses and he became a great leader of the Israelites.

This story is about a boy named Samuel. For years his mother had wished to have a son so when Samuel was born she was very happy. She was so happy she asked Eli, the priest, if he would let Samuel help him in God's temple. It was her way of saying thank you to God for giving her a son.

Eli was getting old and could hardly see so he was glad to have Samuel to help him, and Samuel liked helping Eli in the temple.

One night, when the priest and the boy were resting, Samuel heard someone calling him. Thinking it was Eli he ran to him saying:

'Here I am. You called me.'

'I didn't call you,' said Eli. 'Go back and lie down.'

Samuel went back to rest. Then he heard the voice again:

'Samuel.'

'Here I am,' he said to Eli. 'You did call me.'

But Eli still said he had not called Samuel, although Samuel was quite sure someone was calling him. He was certain of this when he heard the voice a third time and then Eli knew it must be God who was calling Samuel.

'Go and lie down,' he said, 'and if you hear the call again say:

' "Speak, Lord, for your servant is listening." '

Once more Samuel heard the voice. This time he answered as Eli had told him, and God gave him a message about Eli. Now Eli and Samuel both knew that God was calling the boy to become a prophet in Israel.

As Samuel grew older he received more and more messages from God and he became one of God's greatest religious leaders.

In the next story we shall read how Samuel anointed the first king of Israel. Later, he anointed David as the second and greatest king of Israel.

1 SAMUEL, *chapter 3*

Saul–First King of Israel

After Samuel had become known as a prophet, or a seer, the Israelites began asking him to give them a king.

Samuel spoke to God about this.

'About this time tomorrow,' God told him, 'I will send you a man from the land of Benjamin. Anoint him leader over my people Israel.'

Now a man named Saul was travelling around the country looking for his father's lost donkeys. He was from the tribe of Benjamin and was a fine-looking man, taller than any of the others in his tribe. For three days he and his servant travelled from place to place, but they could not find the donkeys. At last Saul said to his servant:

'Let's go back or my father will start worrying about us.'

But the servant had a better idea.

'In this town there is a man of God and everything he says comes true. Perhaps if we find him he will tell us where to look.'

'But we've nothing to give him,' said Saul.

'I have some money,' replied the servant.

So they started off in search of the man of God. On the way they asked some girls where they could find him.

'He's just come into the town,' they said. 'Hurry, and you'll find him before he goes to the feast.'

Samuel was just leaving the town as Saul and his servant arrived.

'Would you please tell me where the seer's house is?' asked Saul.

As soon as Samuel saw Saul he knew that this was the man whom God wanted to govern the people.

'I am the seer,' he said. 'Go up ahead of me for today you are to eat with me and in the morning I will talk with you. As for the donkeys, they have been found.'

Samuel had kept a special place for Saul at the feast and he stayed with Samuel that night. Early the next morning Samuel went with Saul to the end of the town.

'Tell your servant to go on. I want to give you a message from God before you leave,' said Samuel.

When the servant had gone ahead Samuel anointed Saul by pouring a flask of oil over his head, saying:

'The Lord has anointed you leader over his inheritance.'

And so Saul became the first King of Israel. Then Samuel told Saul where he would find the donkeys.

1 SAMUEL, *chapters 9, 10*

David–the Shepherd Boy

When it was time to find someone who could follow Saul as king, God sent Samuel to call on a man named Jesse, who lived in Bethlehem. He was the grandson of Ruth, whose story came earlier in this book.

'I have chosen one of Jesse's sons to be king,' said God. 'You are to anoint the one I have chosen.'

So Samuel set off.

One after another of Jesse's sons came before Samuel, but he knew that God had not chosen any of the seven he had seen.

'Are these all the sons you have?' asked Samuel.

'There is still the youngest, but he is tending the sheep,' said Jesse.

Samuel asked Jesse to send for the shepherd boy and as soon as Samuel saw him he knew this was the one God had chosen. His name was David and Samuel anointed him as God had told him to do.

1 SAMUEL, *chapter 16*

David–Harpist and King

David not only looked after the sheep, he also played the harp. Soon after God had chosen him to be king after Saul, a messenger came to Jesse from Saul, who was ill:

'Send me your son, David, who is with the sheep. I want him to play to me.'

David's father gave his son presents to take to the King and David took his harp and went to Saul. He liked David and every time he was ill David played on his harp until the King felt better. Saul liked David so much that he made him one of his armour bearers.

David learned a lot about the duties of the King and many years later, when Saul died, all the tribes of Israel came to David and said:

'You were the one who led Israel on their military campaigns and the Lord said to you: "You shall shepherd my people Israel and you shall become their ruler." '

So David became King of Israel when he was thirty years old.

1 SAMUEL, *chapter 16;* 2 SAMUEL, *chapter 5*

31

Solomon–the Man of Wisdom

David had a son who was named Solomon. As he became older he was known for his great wisdom. He was also popular with the people, for he was a good man. David wanted his son to succeed him as King and a lot of the people wanted this too.

When the time came, David sent for some of his people and said:

'Take your lord's servants with you and set Solomon, my son, on my own mule and take him to be anointed King of Israel. Blow the trumpets and shout, "Long live King Solomon." Then he is to come and sit on my throne and reign in my place.'

The men went and they did as David had told them.

'Long live King Solomon,' they shouted, and there was great joy among all the people. They played their flutes while they followed their new King.

Solomon proved himself worthy to be King. One of the very important things he did during his reign was to build a temple in which people could worship God. He started building it in the fourth year of his reign. It was to be a very beautiful temple. He bought the best materials he could obtain and employed thousands and thousands of the best workmen. Nothing was too good for God's temple and it took seven years to complete.

Solomon was a good and wise King, and it was a truly golden age.

1 KINGS, *chapters 1, 5, 6*

The Widow's Jug of Oil

As the years went by more kings came to the throne and there were more prophets. One of these prophets was Elijah.

While he was God's prophet there was a drought in the land. Food and water were short because there had been no rain for a long time. God told Elijah to go to a place called Zarephath where he would find a widow who would give him food.

When Elijah arrived at Zarephath, he met the woman as God had promised.

'Would you bring me some water in a jar so that I may drink?' asked Elijah.

The woman stopped gathering sticks for her fire and went to get the water, but Elijah called after her:

'And bring me, please, a piece of bread.'

'I don't have any bread,' she said, 'only a handful of flour in a jar and a little oil. I am gathering sticks to make a fire to cook them so that my son and I may eat and die.'

'Don't be afraid,' said Elijah. 'Do as you have said, but first make a cake of bread for me and bring it to me. Then make another for yourself and your son. The jar of flour will not be used up and the jug of oil will not run dry until the day the Lord gives rain on the land.'

The woman believed what Elijah had said. She made the cake of bread for him and there was enough flour and oil left for herself and her son. Every day there was food for them all, as Elijah had said there would be.

It was one of God's miracles.

1 KINGS, *chapter 17*

The Widow's Son Lives Again

Elijah had said that there would be food for the widow and her son as well as for himself, and there was. But some time later the woman came to him in great distress. She was carrying her young son. He had been ill for some time and now he had stopped breathing.

'What do you have against me?' she asked Elijah. 'Did you come to remind me of my sin and kill my son?'

'Give me your son,' said Elijah.

Then Elijah carried the boy up to his room. He laid him on the bed and stretched himself out on him. Three times he did this as he prayed:

'Oh, Lord my God, let this boy's life return to him.'

God heard and answered Elijah's prayer, and when he gave the boy back to his mother she was very happy.

'Now I know that you are a man of God,' she said, 'and the word of God which you speak is the truth.'

1 KINGS, *chapter 17*

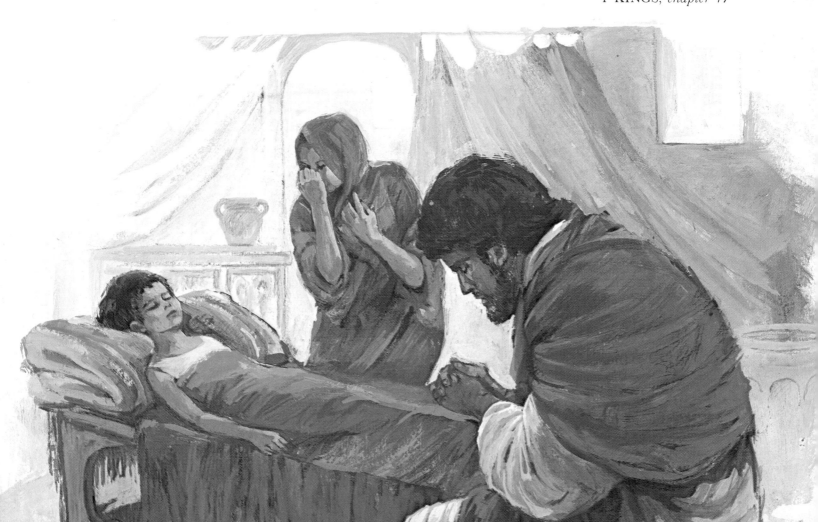

Choose Whom You Will Serve

The reason for the drought in which the widow woman and her son were about to die was that God's people had turned away from him to worship Baal. After three and a half years in which there had been no rain, Elijah went to the wicked King Ahab, who had led God's people astray, and told him:

'You and your people have not followed God's command. You have turned to other gods. Now, get the people together on Mount Carmel and see that all the prophets of the false gods are there.'

Ahab did as Elijah asked and a great crowd of people came together.

'How long will you waver between two opinions?' asked Elijah. 'If the Lord is God follow him, but if Baal is God then follow him.'

Elijah told them to get two bullocks and prepare one of them for sacrifice and he would prepare the other. Then they were to gather wood to make a fire and lay their bullock on it. But they were not to light the wood. Instead they were to call on Baal to light the wood and burn the sacrifice.

There were 450 of Baal's prophets and they did as Elijah told them.

When all was ready they called to Baal to light the wood. All the morning they called, but nothing happened. Then Elijah began to taunt them:

'Shout louder,' he said. 'Perhaps he is in deep thought, or busy, or travelling. Maybe he is asleep and must be awakened!'

So Baal's people shouted louder. They

even cut themselves in their desire that he should answer. But their god did not answer. Nothing happened.

Then, Elijah told the people to gather round him while he prepared *his* bullock. He laid the bullock on the wood but did not light it. He told the people to fill four large jugs with water and pour it over the bullock.

'Do it again,' he said.

And they did.

'Do it a third time,' he said.

And they did.

The water ran over the bullock and filled the trench Elijah had made all round the altar.

Then Elijah stepped forward and prayed.

'Oh, Lord God, let it be known today that you are God and that I am your servant and have done all these things at your command. Answer me, oh Lord God, that these people may know that you, oh Lord God, are God.'

And fire fell from heaven.

The people turned to God and before they could get home black clouds formed, the wind blew and a great rain descended on the thirsty land.

1 KINGS, *chapter 18*

Go–Wash in the River

A little Israelite slave girl was captured when the Syrians were at war with Israel. She was not unhappy in Syria for she had a good mistress who was the wife of Naaman, the commander of the Syrian army. But she was sad because her master was a leper. So one day she said to her mistress:

'If only my master would see the prophet Elisha, who is in Samaria. He would cure him of his leprosy.'

When Naaman heard this he went to the King of that country and told him what the slave girl had said.

'By all means go,' said the King, 'and I will send a letter to the King of Israel.'

So Naaman went. He took with him a lot of expensive presents and his master's letter:

'With this letter I am sending my servant Naaman to you so that you may cure him

of his leprosy,' the King wrote.

But when the King of Israel read the letter he was frightened. He thought the other King was trying to pick a quarrel with him.

'Does he think I am God?' he asked. 'Why does this man send someone to me to be cured of his leprosy?'

But when Elisha heard this, he sent a message asking that Naaman be sent to him.

Naaman went, but he was angry when Elisha sent messengers to say:

'Go wash yourself in the Jordan seven times and you will be cleansed.'

Naaman did not wash in Jordan but started back to his own country.

'Our rivers are better than any of the rivers of Israel,' he said. 'Why couldn't I wash in them and be cured?'

But his servants were wiser than he was.

'If the prophet had told you to do some great thing you would have done it,' they said.

Naaman knew they were right, so he went back and washed in the river Jordan as Elisha had told him, and he was cured.

He was so pleased that he went back to Elisha and said:

'Now I know there is no God in all the world except the God of Israel.'

But when he offered the prophet the presents he had brought, Elisha would not take them.

2 KINGS, *chapter 5*

Isaiah's Prophecies about Jesus

There is a lot about prophets in the Old Testament. Isaiah is one of the best known. He was a major prophet and he prophesied for forty years. He had many visions in that time and he saw God in these. In one of his earlier visions he heard the voice of God saying:

'Whom shall I send? And who will go for us?'

'Here am I. Send me,' said Isaiah.

Then God gave him messages for his people.

Isaiah lived a very long time before Jesus was born but one of the most important messages God gave him was that he would send Jesus into the world, so Isaiah told the people of Israel that God would give them a

sign by sending the baby Jesus to live in the world.

'For unto us a child is born,' Isaiah said, 'unto us a son is given. And the government will be upon his shoulders, and he will be called wonderful, counsellor, mighty God, everlasting Father, Prince of Peace.'

And all this happened in God's good time with the coming of Jesus on the first Christmas morning. Isaiah also foretold the death of Jesus.

The prophets were men who listened to what God had to say to them and Isaiah listened a lot which was why he was able to tell people about Jesus long before he came. He also told how John the Baptist would come to prepare the way for Jesus.

People usually listened to what the prophets had to say and believed them. But when they warned people that they would be punished for the wrong things they did, the prophets were not so popular. The next story is about one who was not popular.

ISAIAH

The Potter and the Clay

Jeremiah, like Isaiah, was one of the major prophets. He prophesied about one hundred years after Isaiah. Today we often say to people who look on the dark side of life, 'Don't be a Jeremiah.' Which is another way of saying, 'Cheer up. Life is not all dreary.'

But there is a dark side of life for those who do not obey God, as we see by what happened in this story.

Jeremiah lived at a time when the people of Israel, the nation which God had led out of captivity, had turned away from God and were doing wrong. As a prophet Jeremiah knew they would suffer for this and it was his duty to warn them of the disasters they would meet.

One day Jeremiah went down to the house of the potter. He watched as the potter took the clay and worked at his wheel to mould it into shape. But the clay did not take

shape as the potter wanted. It was not as he had intended it to be, so he started again, moulding it into a shape that was pleasing.

Jeremiah told this story to the people of Israel to help them to understand that they were like the clay in the hands of the potter, who was like God. He could not mould them into something good because they did not want to do his bidding. They had turned away from him and gone their own way. So Jeremiah warned them that a disaster could come upon them, unless they repented.

'So turn from your evil ways and actions, each one of you,' said Jeremiah, 'for if you repent of your evil ways, then God will not allow these disasters to come upon you.'

But the people would not listen and they put Jeremiah in the stocks.

Jeremiah's prophecy was true. The Babylonians conquered the Israelites and took them into exile away from their own land.

JEREMIAH, *chapter 18*

The Docile Lions

Daniel had been taken from Judea to Babylon as an exile when he was a boy. Now he was eighty years old, and a brave and a wise man, as he had been all his life.

When Darius became King of the Babylonians he appointed 120 men to be the governors of different parts of the country, with three of them in charge of all the rest. Daniel was one of these three. He was the best of them all and the King thought so highly of him that he decided to put him in charge of the whole kingdom.

This made the other men jealous and angry. They tried to find fault with him so that they could persuade the King not to set him over them, but they could not find any fault in him. So they plotted together and then went to see the King.

'We have agreed that you should issue an order that anyone who prays to any god or man during the next thirty days, except to you, oh King, shall be thrown into the lions' den. Now, oh King, put it in writing so that it cannot be altered.'

King Darius was not aware that these men knew Daniel would not obey such an order, so he put the order in writing.

Daniel could have prayed in secret when he knew the fate that would await him if he were seen praying. But he was not that kind of man. Instead, he went to an upstairs room and prayed before an open window which faced Jerusalem. Three times a day he prayed there.

Of course his enemies were watching, and they went straight to the King and told him that Daniel was disobeying his law. The King was very sad. Now he knew what he had done and he tried all day to save Daniel from his fate, but in the end he had to have the law carried out and Daniel was thrown into the lions' den.

'May your God whom you serve continually rescue you,' he said to Daniel.

The King could not sleep that night and he was up early the next morning. He hurried to the lions' den wondering what he would find. Before he got to the place he called out in fear:

'Daniel, has your God been able to save you from the lions?'

To the King's joy Daniel answered:

'My God sent his angel and he shut the mouths of the lions. They have not hurt me.'

Then the King thankfully gave orders for Daniel to be taken out of the lions' den. And there was not one wound on him.

DANIEL, *chapter 6*